Dedication

To god who had faith in me even when I did not. To my mom who let fear run her life. Well fear no more.

For Michael and Aaron's loving support. Kyle my son who has always inspired me since the day he was born.

To Stephen my life partner. To my friend Peter Goldbeck. And a very special thank you to Jose.

Preface

Moments of Belief is about imparting simple yet probing messages. That there is a way out of suffering and it's through Love Compassion and Peace. Each of us has the ability to make a difference every day, to make a direct connection with a higher power for personal transformation so that we can learn how to live life with a real purpose and a real passion.

"I believe one person can make a difference and that is in the Moment of Belief".

Moments of Belief

Michele Oaklander

BALBOA
PRESS
A DIVISION OF HAY HOUSE

Copyright © 2011 Michele Oaklander

All rights reserved. No part of this book may be used or reproduced by any means, graphic, electronic, or mechanical, including photocopying, recording, taping or by any information storage retrieval system without the written permission of the publisher except in the case of brief quotations embodied in critical articles and reviews.

Balboa Press books may be ordered through booksellers or by contacting:

Balboa Press
A Division of Hay House
1663 Liberty Drive
Bloomington, IN 47403
www.balboapress.com
1-(877) 407-4847

Because of the dynamic nature of the Internet, any web addresses or links contained in this book may have changed since publication and may no longer be valid. The views expressed in this work are solely those of the author and do not necessarily reflect the views of the publisher, and the publisher hereby disclaims any responsibility for them.

The author of this book does not dispense medical advice or prescribe the use of any technique as a form of treatment for physical, emotional, or medical problems without the advice of a physician, either directly or indirectly. The intent of the author is only to offer information of a general nature to help you in your quest for emotional and spiritual well-being. In the event you use any of the information in this book for yourself, which is your constitutional right, the author and the publisher assume no responsibility for your actions.

Any people depicted in stock imagery provided by Thinkstock are models, and such images are being used for illustrative purposes only.
Certain stock imagery © Thinkstock.

Printed in the United States of America

ISBN: 978-1-4525-3665-1 (sc)
ISBN: 978-1-4525-3666-8 (hc)
ISBN: 978-1-4525-3667-5 (e)

Library of Congress Control Number: 2011911789

Balboa Press rev. date: 7/18/2011

Table of Contents

The Message 1

In The Flow 2

Your True Self 3

Believe In Yourself 4

Moments of Belief 5

What's In It For Me 6

Road Blocks 7

Manifesting 8

Practice 9

What's Really Important? 10

How Do I Start 11

Having a Clear Vision 12

A Mindful Plan 13

On Your Way 14

A Celebration 15

Strong Emotions Held Within 16

Changing One's Ways 17

Decisions of The Heart 18

When A Door Closes 19

Love of Money 20

Waiting for an Answer 21

Heirs to Our Success 22

Intellectual Games 23

The Strange New Way of Becoming Your Own Friend 24

Self-Destructive Worries 25

Love What You Do. 26

Pastime. 27

The Joyful Encounter of Mastering a Situation.... 28

Turning One's Goals into Reality. 29

Joys of the Heart 30

Knowing When to Step Aside 31

Completion of a Task 32

Unsolvable Dilemmas 33

Turning Ones Goals into Reality with Endurance and Consistency . .34

Self-Confident Manner 35

A Solution for Disputes 36

Becoming Aware of Your Possibilities. 37

Staying Committed 38

Accepting Yourself 39

Aha 40

Steps to a New Beginning 41

Capable Manager 42

Assertive Will 43

A Spiritual Experience 44

Nightmares 45

Inner Pulses 46

Self-Control 47

Change of Luck 48

A New Development. 49

A Change of Perspective 50

The Enjoyment of Taking a Risk 51

Love Yourself. 52

Trusting the Inner Voice 53

Deep Happiness 54

Starting at Zero 55

Clearing of the Way 56

Something New 57

Despite Fears. 58

Express Yourself 59

Solid Work. 60

Don't Avoid the Conflict 61

The Connection 62

Intuitive Advisor 63

A Relaxed Soul 64

Strong Enterprising Spirit 65

Laws of Growth 66

Teamwork 67

Taking Your Place 68

Crossing A Threshold 69

Using Your Power 70

Promises 71

Dependable Me 72

Logic. 73

The Sureness of Instinct 74

The Removal of Stagnation. 75

My Own Suggestions 76

Clear Solutions. 77

Crystallization 78

Inhibitions 79

A Fresh Start 80

Dance of Joy 81

Ready for Action 82

Focus. 83

The Light 84

Loving Feelings 85

Exploration 86

Stay Persistent 87

Trust and Faith. 88

Serenity 89

Your Success 90

Ambition. 91

Smart Enough to Hear 92

Artistic Inspiration 93

Gateway 94

Creative Spirit 95

Charge 96

Freelance 97

Heaven and Earth 98

Creative Force 99

Decisive Willpower 100

Joining Forces 101

Focused Attention 102

New Vision 103

Reaching the Goal 104

The Hand of Fate 105

Connecting to Spirit 106

A New Kind of Hope 107

Wide Awake 108

Fulfillment 109

Path to Wholeness 110

Strong Character 111

A Successful Development 112

Shadows 113

The Important Step 114

Shift of Luck 115

A Relaxation 116

Bold Adventures 117

Good News 118

Pioneer Work 119

Inside Out 120

Solid Progress 121

The Change 122

Joining Forces 123

Responsible Position 124

The Message

This is my first blog post and what I am about to tell you started over the summer of July 2010. It seems to just happen one day it just started coming through. This is as said to me I did not change anything

Death Azarel: I feel you want me to teach people how and why to live. I don't mean go through the motions but really start to live, feel, love so that when it is time to go, and we all have to go that you will truly feel ready, so many go with regret, worry, shame, guilt, fear illness, disease, pity stop this people love yourself love your life, live every day in spirit. Love harmony don't let worry, doubt, depression get you down, rob you of life. This is your experience, so experience it to the fullest, find people who want to live like you, to the fullest, connect grow create with each other.

The channeling has not stopped there is more? I have also been instructed to write a book.

In The Flow

Being in the flow of how things work, how energy moves is just the beginning for some people they will just be in that state. Others will go deeper, and pull out something new even for those already in the know these are the people changing things.

Your True Self

Do whatever it is you have to do to find your true self your higher self, as you lose your false self you will also lose your false friends.

Believe In Yourself

You must start asking yourself if it does not work towards a goal then why? Believe in the power of your ability to perceive a goal, and then your way to that goal, even through the difficult parts.

Moments of Belief

Moments of Belief are when you start to believe in yourself, in the life force, the source that there is something greater than yourself. It's that split second realization flash in the pan is all one needs sometimes to go on, to make it though. Like an epiphany it can hit us without warning, and then we just know. These are Moments of Belief.

What's In It For Me

You need to stop worrying about what you're getting! You need to start caring instead, about what you may be able to give to another. Your heart is in the future, looking out for your best interests and the people you care about. All you need to do is follow. Follow your heart.

Road Blocks

Stop blocking yourself. Squash that voice that tells you no or that you can't do it. Don't listen to the Debbie Downers. Find the support people that you need in life. They may not always be your family or your closest friends; it could be someone from another culture, background, or faith. You should be open to all people and things in life. Each one of us has something to offer if we just open our hearts and listen.

Manifesting

Be patient! Know that every step you take is building a new consciousness of abundance and will appear on the outside as a new circumstance and/or condition. Give thanks and appreciation for all you have, for this will make you a magnet to more.

Practice

You need to practice what you are learning to experience the fruits of your work. Be open to new ideas. Trust and believe in yourself. Let yourself and not others be the authority of what is right for you. Embrace whatever happens!

What's Really Important?

When was the last time you asked yourself what is really important? Now have the wisdom and courage that is needed to build your day, your life around your answer.

How Do I Start

How does one start a new beginning? One step at a time, the greatest cause of worry is fear. Your first step in conquering fear is to learn not to be frightened of fear itself. It's the change of things that scare us. Not knowing what to expect, this is where you really need to be aware of old patterns, so you don't find yourself repeating the same things like they are brand new but in a different way. The ego is very good at convincing us that we are on a new path, but over time we are soon let down. So embrace fear and realize that it is the door to change.

Having a Clear Vision

Set a goal, get a plan, map it out and stick to it. Believe in the power of your ability to perceive a goal and then your way to that goal, even through the difficult parts. Commend yourself.

A Mindful Plan

Rewards are earned by those with the vision to see beyond the temporary, as you embrace the benefits of a productive and mindful plan. Believe in yourself for you have the power.

On Your Way

Know that you are always taken care of by your guardian angel everyday so even when you are faced with conflicts and disputes know that they are by your side. Be open to sudden and radical changes. Look at endings as new beginnings and don't shy away from the strangeness of it. Remain alert and focus on the details. For then you will have success.

A Celebration

When you are in a reflective state this can be most liberating, the process of looking inward will allow you to change your mind. Understanding the big picture will allow you to be patience. Looking into matters is the key to removing confusion and delusion, as well as being able to dissolve boundaries. Therefore you will not feel like you are trapped, whether in reality you are or not.

Strong Emotions Held Within

When you have close observation of yourself while searching for the truth this often will create an exchange of criticism in oneself. This is when you need to remember to have love and compassion for yourself and realize that this is the way to a victory.

Changing One's Ways

Trusting one's feelings in everyday life through self-reliance and creatively taking concrete steps. This will allow a state of balance in resolving conflicts.

Decisions of The Heart

When you make a heartfelt decision this is true courage and willpower, to see your committed plans through. The successful connection between your intuition and knowledge. Through the chaos and loss we can find balance between passion and harmony.

When A Door Closes

Sudden and radial changes can motivate a change for new projects. With faith and discretion you can expertly arrival at a safe, confident place without excessive trust in others. This is a complete change of opinion.

Love of Money

When working with a higher power and authority one can expand and see the fruits of ones labor. Having a control on materialism will uncover plots and tough competition that we face each day called envy, low self-esteem and jealousy which create a profound unease in us. Realizing this is a resolution to a problem.

Waiting for an Answer

When a new horizon opens up for you to learn or teach something don't be afraid, for it gives you a chance to change your mind and learn something about yourself. Each of you is a star and we are here to co-create your story.

Heirs to Our Success

Awards of success should be given to ourselves for the expansion of the work. When we work in alliance with our self we allow the inner self a voice. This then becomes the higher self and that is when we can have a true religious celebration.

Intellectual Games

Being aware of our own inner and outer wealth allows us to patiently trust in the natural cycles of life. When we are inspired by our feelings, insight into totality which includes opposites can be realized and that a truce doesn't always mean peace. This is how we can start to consciously experience inner peace and harmony.

The Strange New Way of Becoming Your Own Friend

We need to remember to stop and reward ourselves for our success. When we take a closer look at ourselves through our own observations, only then can we see the real courage and confidence that has brought us to this moment of personal care and foresight.

Self-Destructive Worries

When we block our development with the "fear of life" we are creating a "straitjacket" for our self. It then makes our lives difficult, because of the new distraction. When we use our thirst for knowledge, we have an opportunity to clarify some issues using our inner guidance. We can then hope for good prospects and trust in the future. This can bring about a change for the better.

Love What You Do

When we become mature enough to achieve our objective of joy and abundnce we allow our self a victory a reward. Threw logic and spiritual nourishment the natural cycles of change can happen, therefore opening the doors of destiny.

Pastime

When we have short lived quarrels within our self, it takes a certain amount of courage and hard work to straighten these issues out. Through long term commitments to our self and family we can take charge of the administration of fate and really step through the doors of the proud and noble.

The Joyful Encounter of Mastering a Situation...

When we let time work for us, we are having a deep experience of meaning. This allows us a chance to develop a trust in one's own abilities, securing and anchoring what has already been achieved. Decisive, goal-oriented, and courageous actions.

Turning One's Goals into Reality

When we are able to have faith in the unknown this can begin the undertaking of intuitive suggestions, leading us away from servitude. So celebrate when they occur!

Joys of the Heart

With the expansion of consciousness while searching for the truth we can start to see an increase in our awareness of security and power. This can start a rebellion in us that brings about a healthy sense of self-assurance. By allowing the light in us, we can have equilibrium.

Knowing When to Step Aside

When you are forced to let go, calling for a truce is a temporary retreat. Sometimes understanding the natural growth process and perceiving one's own dependencies, we can free our self from them. So that you can take responsibility and concentrate completely on the things you are in charge of.

Completion of a Task

Understand that constantly avoiding conflicts practically cause strife. To reach your goals you must remain ambitious to the challenge, with stable values. The reward for this accomplished effort is determination and a renewal in hope.

Unsolvable Dilemmas

When you decide to overcome inner tensions, and find a way out of an unsolvable dilemma you start to draw a clear line. Trusting in the future with hope as your guidance, you can enjoy a rich relationship. When you become aware of the disruptive fields that hinder one's own will you to take an optimistic approach to life with self-assurance.

Turning Ones Goals into Reality with Endurance and Consistency

When you turn your projects into reality, you grow beyond your own limitations. Through the power of conviction we can enjoy what has been achieved, using one's means and possibilities in a responsible manner. When you follow your goals without letting rebounds cause confusion a favorable interplay of forces can create a new development.

Self-Confident Manner

When you open up emotionally and express concealed feeling and desires this will allow you to follow your goal's. By opening up to an unwelcome but totally necessary insight into the transient and threatening aspects of life, you can learn to finally let go.

A Solution for Disputes

In order to have a stable relationship you must treat each other carefully, and maintain a responsible position. When you struggle with difficulties, you must take a leap of faith and try to successful work it out together. Sometimes changing ones ways means recognizing one's own errors. You must look to the future with a spirit of trust in each other.

Becoming Aware of Your Possibilities

You have every right to feel confident within yourself, and enjoy the fruits of your labor. Try something new, stop clinging to familiar ideas. Be guided by destiny, and find your true calling. Let something mature in you, use this opportunity to find great happiness.

Staying Committed

When you forge ahead with insight and perception, you learn to differentiate between the goal and the addiction. Proceeding in an independent and clever way, allows you to stand up for a plan of action. Making a conscious decision about life, is taking a risk, but it can produce visible results.

Accepting Yourself

Finding the right emotional balance within yourself can avoid deception. When you are open to your emotions you are taking a great step towards the goal. By celebrating the occasions when they occur, you create a harmonious link within yourself. When you become inflamed about something, you can start to appreciate the relationship that you have with your higher self.

Aha

Recognize that self-fulfillment requires a willingness to take the initiative, learn to listen to your inner voice and trust it. When you don't allow yourself to express your feelings you block your development. It's about fulfillment, deep gratitude, and trusting that everything will go well.

Steps to a New Beginning

Drawing on your own unlimited resources today, allows you to be adaptable to your own persistent energy. When you can't remain focused you dissipate your energy, it then becomes very easy to wind up in a sea of deception. Opening up to the mysteries of love and happiness will encourage you to take action without hesitation, purposefully and decisively.

Capable Manager

With your own natural force you can create, a momentum of a high velocity of energy that will fuel itself as you approach your goal. This is a manifestation. When your energy is in balance a sense of calmness comes over you, this will allow you the power and ambition to stay open to inspiration, intuition, and intelligence.

Assertive Will

When sudden solutions to problems become flashes of inspiration, let yourself be guided by your inner voice. Trusting in your own abilities to master a situation allows you to take responsibility and focus on the things you are in charge of, your growth and creativity. You just might walk right into the arms of happiness. It's about love and devotion to yourself.

A Spiritual Experience

When you connect with others in a loving way, it becomes your personal responsibility to up hold that. Taking the initiative in the joys of life, allows you the courage to be responsible and persistent in your own self-development. Coming out of the fog and finding fulfillment is just the beginning. It's the start of shattering restrictive beliefs.

Nightmares

By maintaining a sober perception about your clarity, you can balance out the nightmares and negative thinking. Seeing things through, turns goal's into reality. Don't get sidestepped in dogma, prejudices, or negative ideas. Learn to overpower fear and worry that can lead you to panic. Encounter your inner animal and tame it with love.

Inner Pulses

With the birth of success you can become inspired by a goal that's within reach. Your high spirits and hopefulness about the new beginning can fuel a commitment. Starting off into the unknown with careful foresight is a skill necessary for the growth process.

Self-Control

Having the insight to know when to let go of something so it can end naturally, is your use of clarity and knowledge. As you long for the union of hope and harmony, you start to develop a deep insight and trust into the cosmic laws, this allows you to build up your strength while you standstill.

Change of Luck

When you allow yourself to grow beyond your limitations, you sometimes create a threat within yourself. Through innovative thinking you can look to the future and develop a trust in spirit. By not giving up on yourself, you let innovative ideas through that urge their expression. This is cooperation and trust in teamwork.

A New Development

When a disturbance comes along that you least expected, self-fulfillment will require taking a risk. Your eagerness to fight adversity can bring meaning to the experience. By placing your confidence in the divine you can remain open to change and wait for a new direction.

A Change of Perspective

In order to welcome a new development you must realize that time has run out on your old restrictions. Having a sense of security with a higher force, allows you to encounter life in an open and confident way. By opening yourself up to a new perception and taking immediate action, you can become involved in a plan with all your heart.

The Enjoyment of Taking a Risk

There comes a time in your life, when you must put a stop to something. After much apprehension you can begin a plan with courage and commitment. Realizing that your endurance is necessary to workout clear concepts. The amount of stress and pressure is part of the self-sacrifice. Trusting your feelings in everyday life, can produce visible results as a payment for all the work done.

Love Yourself

When you try to force something by all means this can interfere with the divine plan of things. This defeats the lesson that you are to learn. You will know when it's time to take a new path, a more promising path, by remaining flexible and open to pleasant changes. When you retire from participation in these events, you can let something mature in you.

Trusting the Inner Voice

When you overcome fear there is a period of helplessness. This is when your true leadership qualities and strong will must prevail. The process can be difficult because of distractions, self-doubt and slip ups but the change for the better will be worth it. With stable values and a straight forward approach with perseverance there is an opportunity to find fulfillment.

Deep Happiness

Taking a great leap forward towards a goal is being true to yourself. When you successfully complete something meaningful this allows you to open up to a new development and carefully advance. By setting a new trend for the future you can decide, what is essential and define your position. It's about taking your place and enjoying life.

Starting at Zero

You can easily set right whatever has been upside down by patiently trusting in the natural cycles of life. Don't become confused under pressure. Recognize where you played your role in it, and give it your best to overcome the contradictions. This allows you to prevent a one sidedness that can lead you down a dead end street. You should strive for a fair and balanced solution.

Clearing of the Way

Opening up to an unwelcome but totally necessary insight, can expose you to your deceptions and addictions. With self-assurance, you can succeed at bringing differences together that appeared to be insurmountable. By becoming aware of the disruptive things that distract you and create inner conflict. With strong self-confidence and high spirits you can have success, and bring order into your everyday life.

Something New

When your viewing something objectively and soberly, this allows you to succeed in taking definitive steps. You feel strong knowing exactly what you want. By bringing the light into the darkness, you can follow your inner urges. With a deep insight and trust in the cosmic laws, you can build on stability and structure for the future.

Despite Fears

It's about successfully completing something and showing yourself some gratitude. By having the self confidence in knowing what you want, you can reach your goals. Be happy about optimism, make something of it. When you are willing to take on a challenge with an eagerness about it a sense of emotional security can come over you. Now with an impulsive desire for adventure you can live life in a spontaneous way.

Express Yourself

When you make a heartfelt decision about a plan that you have been hesitate about until now, this can put back the momentum into something that has been weighted down. If you can recognize what has kept you trapped, you have an excellent chance of liberating yourself. By opening up yourself to new perceptions, and then taking immediate action. You can see things through and turn your goals into a reality. When you take control of your power you bring structure and clarity to a confused matter.

Solid Work

When you have a painful perception about yourself this can create a feeling of insecurity. By welcoming new developments, you can overcome inner conflicts. Through self-liberation you can do your best to overcome the contradictions. When you make peace with yourself, you can bring together the differences.

Don't Avoid the Conflict

Through the joy of experimentation, and the ability to explore the unknown areas of our self, you can recognize your destiny and shape your tasks in life around it. By taking the time to really enjoy the moment, and the opportunity to understand your patterns in it. Through self-examination while searching for the meaning behind it all you can encounter your shadow. By getting to the bottom of things, you can learn to stand up for yourself and no longer have to retreat from life's experiences.

The Connection

When you decide to release the fear of loss, you know longer become entangled in the nightmares. By opening up to the mysteries of all en-compassing love you can begin to have deep spiritual experiences, like a form of isolation. Through this process you can bring about endurance and persistence to successfully master your goals.

Intuitive Advisor

Using an opportunity for finding great happiness can sometimes be fates way of forcing your happiness on you. How you experience the coming period of time is up to you, are you willing to open up to your destiny? Trusting in life's force for growth, allows you to seize this opportunity when it comes along. Realize that the calm doesn't mean that the storm won't break. By trusting in the meaning of life itself, you will have the opportunity to realize the values that are truly important to you.

A Relaxed Soul

When you become aware of how easy it is for you to become seduced, you no longer avoid confrontations even at the risk of losing time. By bring the light into the darkness you can maintain your devotion to a goal. This shows courage and your passion in the fulfillment of it. Be ready for surprises, open up to impulses. Celebrate your good relationship with the universe.

Strong Enterprising Spirit

By taking the initiative to mastering your tasks, you can take the first steps towards your heartfelt goals. When you let feelings of worry and panic takeover, you are not able to meet your challenges. By having a stable sense of emotional security, you can draw on your wealth of ideas with a presence of mind. It's about taking a risk on your own behalf.

Laws of Growth

When you become aware of your wealth and rest on your laurels, you can give wings to your soul. By using the opportunity to put things in order you can break out of constrictive concepts and structures that have kept you imprisoned. Playing with thoughts and curious questioning can bring honesty about yourself instead of having to pretend. This can spare you from unpleasant experiences in the future.

Teamwork

By looking for what is substantial you can develop a high-level of work ethics. Through innovative thinking you can explore areas of the unknown. With a good plan you can have a new beginning, be ready for action, develop a pioneer spirit allow yourself to grow beyond your comfort zone. Take a risk. Understand inner guidance and let yourself be found.

Taking Your Place

When you finally unblock your emotions and allow yourself to be fulfilled, you can reach a level of success in yourself that comes from invoked thoughts. By realizing that you have the confidence and ability to push forward, you can put your fears to rest once and for all, you can welcome the change.

Crossing A Threshold

By laying down the foundation for long term goals, which are important to you. Realize that making well considered decision; unambiguous decisions are your true power. Don't let self-destructive worries turn into nightmares. Put to rest your fears. Become inspired by a goal that is now within your reach.

Using Your Power

By taking the initiative to enjoy life you have the opportunity for self-fulfillment. When you become firm with disruptive influences, goals know longer become doubts and inner conflicts. By changing your luck for the better, you can become aware of your possibilities. Taking a new direction will change your way of thinking, realize that you must tear down in order to build up.

Promises

When you open up to a new adventure, be ready to take the big leap. Realize that you are taking concrete steps toward a new beginning. When you confidently find self-fulfillment you can then, recognize why it is a smart move.

Dependable Me

In order to make this day a success and everyday a success, you must have faith and confidence in yourself. When you become aware of your goals, and grow beyond your limits this allows you to become proud of yourself. By staying devoted and inspired you can find a state of balance within. When you let go of fear, you can start to rely upon yourself.

Logic

Realize that when you make an intelligent decision it's the beginning of changing your destiny. Innovate solutions to problems can come to you as flashes of inspiration. By learning to trust your gut instincts you can experience life to its fullest. Then you can finally let go of the fear of failure.

The Sureness of Instinct

When you learn to take a risk in life seriously, and without getting discouraged along the way you can then face deception. By drawing on your abundant resources you can experience a vital flow of energy. This will instinctively aid you in doing the right thing. Finding the right balance through self-assurance can bring on a dynamic team spirit.

The Removal of Stagnation

With balanced and peaceful feelings you can lay to rest the worrying and helplessness. Having the knowledge and clarity to see the transformation within yourself, can bring about a great sense of happiness. Your unconscious forces are at work again.

My Own Suggestions

With self- liberation you can release the awakening spirit that strives for something higher. When you are farsighted and confident you can then look to the horizons. By remaining passionately devoted to your goals a sense of great fulfillment can overcome you, sending calamity on its way. It's about following your heart and making a clear decision too.

Clear Solutions

By taking a cautious approach to your goals you let time work for you. Take the time to make the decisions that need to be made and avoid unclear situations. When you allow yourself to open up to a new approach in life, you can get rid of what is outdated. By understanding your decisions you can work on genuine solutions.

Crystallization

By opening up to the joys in your life you can open up to inspiration. Dedicate yourself to your goals, by not letting rebounds or confusion get in the way. Realize your limits and act responsibly, trust in the approaching future with hope.

Inhibitions

By reaching for the top in life you can create your own luck. Don't underestimate yourself, clear up things that should have been cleared up long ago. By focusing on your dreams, you have so many reasons to celebrate.

A Fresh Start

With good ideas and new projects, you can create an individualistic approach to life. When you realize what you need to change, you can then make the necessary sacrifices to achieve and enjoy something of value. Do what you have to do.

Dance of Joy

When you become aware of the unlimited amount of possibilities available, you can begin to brainstorm. By forging ahead passionately you can organize thoughts as future possibilities. Become inspired by the goals that are within your reach. Work in a self-confident, goal-oriented manner.

Ready for Action

By finding fulfillment in your goals, you can create a desire for adventure. When you maintain the highest perception you can avoid fears, before the important step. Realize it's about finding your calling and reaching the goal.

Focus

While you are successfully completing your goal, have the courage and willpower to become inflamed about it. When you set a new momentum you encourage success. With disappointment and sorrow at bay, you can be sure that you are at the development stage of creativity.

The Light

By reawakening your spirits, you can have an emotional recovery. When you fear life, you block your development. By trusting in the future, with a higher guidance you can have steady continuous progress. When you go to the depths of your emotions, you can finally see what has oppressed you for so long and put an end to it.

Loving Feelings

When you become aware of your self-confidence you can then take the initiative, realize that self-fulfillment will require you to take some risks. By having the courage to forge ahead you can easily recognize old patterns and stale ideas. With a garantee of security and the desire to work towards your commitments, you can put your trust in team spirit.

Exploration

You must become aware of the responsibilities that have developed from your new beginnings. When you expand your world views, you can begin with gratitude, by moving on to new horizons. This will bring in the right mixture of progress.

Stay Persistent

By liberating yourself of what has become constritive, you can finally find fulfillment. Don't hesitate to take the initiative be willing to take a risk or two, have a desire for a victory. By working in a confident and self-reliant way you can show your leadership abilities. Give birth to your creative and intuitive power.

Trust and Faith

You must put to rest the avoidance of conflict. By changing your ways of handling issues, you can lay to rest the failure of your projects. When you maintain a strong sense of security, you can avoid disappointment.

Serenity

By taking responsibility for your goals, you create a leadership role that sends you off in new directions. The willingness to be guided is starting off into the unknown, to find true happiness and fulfillment.

Your Success

Through your painful perceptions of the past, you can now have a impetuous new beginning. When you start to fulfill new goals, you can cross over the threshold of fear. By listening to your inner voice and trusting it you, can let destiny waltz right in.

Ambition

When you decide to make a clean sweep of all your dishearten thoughts your true leadership abilities can shine through. By making a heartfelt decision you can make a sensible and clear decision that brings about a charged atmosphere.

Smart Enough to Hear

By remaining calm and stable, you can experience a sense of security. Staying devoted to the goal, can keep you in a state of balance. Knowing when to be ambitious and aggressive, is knowing when to listen to your inner voice. It's a promising new beginning.

Artistic Inspiration

When you consciously and willingly let go of outdated issues, you can move towards new goals. Become inspired by new ideas. Enjoy life for the moment, and harvest what one has sown. With insight into the bigger picture, you can work on lucrative prospects.

Gateway

By overcoming your difficulties you can reward yourself for a successful conclusion to your problems. Taking the opportunity to find fulfillment has brought about a change in your way of thinking. By trusting your intuition, you now don't mind waiting to be guided.

Creative Spirit

When you realize the first step has been taken this will show that things are in a state of balance. When you become aware of the possibilities, you can develop your confidence. By using your imagination you can think outside the box, for you are a wealth of ideas.

Charge

By putting the past to rest you open up yourself to a new task that demands intuition and imagination. Let this be a turning point, so you can draw on an abundant source of inspiration. By following your heart's desire with ambition and aggressive actions.

Freelance

As you gain a new level of success, you can start to search for new ideas and a new independence. Successfully working with intuition and knowledge, you can bring about a strategic calculation that can change your direction. Have the courage and strength to take life by the reins.

Heaven and Earth

By concentrating on your goals, you can experience a positive flow of energy. Remain flexible and intelligence enough to let inspiration flow through. Despite all your fears, you are about to have your success.

Creative Force

When you have doubt, you make it difficult for intuition to progress. Don't you let your thoughts get ahead of you, for this could cause you to end up with deceptive hopes. Though courage and the willingness to a take risk, you can let time work on building something for you.

Decisive Willpower

By finding fulfillment in your success, you can let go of the threatening aspects of life. When you follow your goals and having faith in the future, you dissolve many of the distractions. This will keep disappointment and sorrow away.

Joining Forces

By opening the door to your creative power, and allowing the mental clarity to shine through you can successfully fulfilled your goals. You're ability to stay inspired by ideas can bring about a fair compromise. It's a new beginning.

Focused Attention

Sometimes taking a risk is just what is needed to put conflicts into a state of balance. When you work harmoniously with your intuition you can develop a happy relationship. Your successful connection with intuition and knowledge can bring about a ecstasy of high spirits.

New Vision

With a new and promising outlook on the future and consistently working towards your goals. This has brought you to suddenly realize that there are certain aspects of yourself that you are being forced to let go. By maintaining a sober perception to what happens next, you can easily break away and make a nice clean sweep.

Reaching the Goal

By remaining full of gratitude you can reached a level of fulfillment that is joyful. When you refuse to give into the disillusions and weaknesses you can bring about an independent presence of mind. This can show you the next steps in the right direction that will require you to take the initiative.

The Hand of Fate

By following though with your actions, you can now harvest what you sow. Your wealth of ideas have crossed a threshold. Bringing you to an emotionally fulfilling state, that can encourage growth and creativity to build something together.

Connecting to Spirit

In reaching your goals you have struggled with many difficulties and taken many risks. Through clever maneuvers you have started off into the unknown, while hatching new concepts and taking care of what has been entrusted to you. This has brought about a new favorable development.

A New Kind of Hope

When you suddenly realize that you can intellectually unblock development, this can bring a new meaning to emotional security. By having trust in the divine, you can develop a world of visible manifestations.

Wide Awake

By consistently working towards a goal that has been set into motion, you have an opportunity for a lasting success. When you overcome obstacles with decisions from the heart you create opportunities for growth and new developments. Realize that when you are in a fertile stage, that you don't have to worry about nothing working out.

Fulfillment

When you remain calm and composed you can work through your most difficult task at hand. By putting your self-doubts and fears into a state of balance you then become aware of your possibilities, confidence and success.

Path to Wholeness

When you single-handily take on problems you run the risk of frustration, that nothing is going to work out. By finding your center you can eliminate your feeling of concern and panic. Allow yourself to open up to the all-compassing love, so you can find joy and fulfillment in what you do.

Strong Character

Through the liberation of yourself, success and self-confidence have forged the way for promising plans in the future. By eliminating the resistance, and getting rid of the contradictions you can make progress. When you instinctively follow your calling and maintain trust in the future you can be sure of great joy and fulfillment.

A Successful Development

When you are able to wait for a favorable opprotunity to translate your ideas into reality, the rewards for this accomplished effort are an opportunity for a lasting success. By sending disappointing expectations on their way you can avoid them in the future.

Shadows

By completing your goals you show persistence and concentration, that is what is necessary to achieve a solid success. The rewards for this accomplished effort are no longer having doubt or inner conflicts. With new beginnings you can grow into your creative self.

The Important Step

When you successfully unite forces within yourself, a welcome development of teamwork can appear. By working together through love, you can take the necessary steps. A well-established team, sure instincts and persistent can bring about a meaningful experience.

Shift of Luck

By liberating yourself from the past taking the initiative and mastering your tasks, you have opened yourself up to a new world. Through a stroke of luck your creativity and growth have brought about a happiness that you are about to receive.

A Relaxation

By having an aggressive ambition you can bring a new spirit into your life. Growing beyond your limitations and struggling with your difficulties, can bring about the ability to make well-considered decisions. Confidently look to the future, and let go of the past.

Bold Adventures

With a desire for adventure and delightful developments you can now feel the energy, so let your passions get the best of you. Allow yourself to remain receptive and devoted to your feelings, trust that you will do the right thing. Be guided to your destiny.

Good News

By suddenly realizing your opportunities for success, you can maintain a high spirit about the birth of your success. By finding fulfillment with your progress and insight, you can now have good prospects and trust in the future.

Pioneer Work

When you have patience with yourself, you can bring about a serenity and endurance to your goals. Now with great force and courage you can finally fulfill your goals. By finishing your projects you can now have a calm before the storm.

Inside Out

With the happiness of fateful events you can find fulfillment within your goals. When you remove the disillusion of helplessness, and maintain a mature patient and stable stance disappointing expectations can fade. Keep your hopes up high and trust in the future.

Solid Progress

When unexpected obstacles start to test your patience you can start to feel powerless. By having the mental clarity to break these thoughts off, with the birth of your success. You can clearly see the unconscious forces that are trying to betray you.

The Change

By remaining devoted to my intuition I have achieved my goals. With a hopeful new beginning to a solid success, these transformations have furthered my spiritual development. By having sober perceptions of clarity with high spirits, this has brought me to a culminating point.

Joining Forces

By pushing yourself with a committed action you can begin a plan with courage and commitment. When you find a solution to your problems you can forge ahead with perception and knowlegde by releasing frustration and fear. By allowing yourself to remain flexible you can be clever and brilliant in reaching your goals.

Responsible Position

By cautiously planning a new beginning you can build up your confidence and success realize that you are standing on facts now and must call it a truce. With a happy relationship and trust in teamwork this will be the motivation for a new project.

www.ingramcontent.com/pod-product-compliance
Lightning Source LLC
Chambersburg PA
CBHW020007050426
42450CB00005B/355